DRIBBLE, SHOOT, GROW

Inspiring Basketball Stories to Help Kids Build Life Skills Like Teamwork, Resilience, Creativity, and Persistence

Inspiring Winning Stories

CONTENTS

Introduction   1

Michael Jordan   3

Kobe Bryant   7

Shaquille O'Neal   13

Lebron James   19

Charles Barkley   25

Magic Johnson   29

David Robinson   33

Kareem Abdul-Jabbar   37

Kevin Durant   43

Stephen Curry   47

Steve Nash   51

Larry Bird   55

Tim Duncan   59

Allen Iverson   63

Dirk Nowitzki   67

James Naismith 71

MVP Trophy 75

Slam Dunks 77

Review 79

Introduction

Hello, future all-stars and game-changers of the world! Welcome to "Dribble, Shoot, Grow"

Have you ever watched a game of basketball and found yourself on the edge of your seat, cheering as a player makes a breathtaking shot right at the buzzer? Or felt the thrill of witnessing a gravity-defying slam dunk that stirs up thunderous applause? This isn't just a game; it's a world of grit, determination, soaring triumphs, and lessons learned from missed shots. It's a game that echoes the rhythm of life itself.

In the pages of this book, you'll encounter some of the most remarkable personalities from the thrilling world of basketball. You'll journey through the inspiring lives of legends like Michael Jordan, who taught us that we miss every shot we don't take, and Magic Johnson, who showed us that true magic is making everyone around us better.

You'll meet trailblazers like Dr. James Naismith, the inventor of basketball, who turned a simple idea into a global sport. We'll explore inspiring stories of transformation, like that of Steve Nash, the underestimated athlete who became an MVP through relentless dedication and hard work.

Each of these stories paints a vivid picture of the power of perseverance, teamwork, creativity, and belief. They are stories of individuals who have dribbled, shot, and dunked their way to greatness, but more importantly, they are about the heart, spirit, and passion that drives champions on and off the court.

But this book is not just about the legends of basketball. It's about you! Because within you lies the power to dream, the strength to overcome, and the spirit to achieve. Whether you aspire to be an all-star on the court, or a champion in the game of life, these stories will inspire you to reach for the stars, and remind you that no hurdle is too high, no dream too big.

So, get ready to lace up your shoes and step onto the court of life. Open this book, and let's tip-off on this exciting journey together. Because who knows? The next inspiring basketball story could be yours.

Let the game begin!

MICHAEL JORDAN

Once upon a time, in the small town of Wilmington, North Carolina, a young boy named Michael Jordan dreamed of becoming a basketball player. He idolized the NBA stars on TV, often staying up late to watch games and spending hours practicing shots in his backyard. He was a hard worker but still had a long way to go before becoming a great player.

When Michael was in high school, he tried out for the varsity basketball team. He was a sophomore at the time, and even though he was tall and fast, he was also quite skinny and inexperienced compared to the older boys. When the list of players who made the team was posted, Michael's name was not on it. He was devastated. He went home and cried in the privacy of his room, feeling a pain that was more intense than any physical injury.

But Michael didn't let this setback extinguish his dream. Instead, he turned his disappointment into determination. He used it as fuel to work harder than he ever had before. He joined the junior varsity team and practiced relentlessly, often being the first to arrive and the last to leave.

Over the next year, Michael grew taller, stronger, and more skillful. His tenacity and commitment were unmatched. When it was time to try out for the varsity team again, he was not just ready, but eager. This time, he made the team and quickly distinguished himself as one of the best players.

Fast forward a few years later, Michael Jordan became one of the greatest basketball players in history. He led the Chicago Bulls to six NBA championships and earned five MVP awards. He was known for his competitive nature, his amazing skills, and his ability to perform under pressure.

But, for many, his greatest achievement is not the records he set or the championships he won, but the example he set about the power of perseverance. Michael Jordan once said, "I've missed more than 9000 shots in my career. I've lost almost 300 games. 26 times, I've been trusted to take the game-winning shot and missed. I've failed over and over and over again in my life. And that is why I succeed."

This story about Michael Jordan is a lesson for all of us, especially for kids. It tells us that success is not about never failing, but about getting back up every time we fall. It's about trying our best, giving our all, and never giving up on our dreams, no matter how big or small they might be.

Fun facts:

Space Jam Star: Michael Jordan didn't only play basketball; he was also the star of a popular movie. In 1996, he played himself in the movie "Space Jam," alongside cartoon characters like Bugs Bunny. The film was a big hit and shows kids that you can take your talents to new and unexpected places.

Baseball Player: Did you know that Michael Jordan also played professional baseball? In 1994, after his first retirement from basketball, he played for the Birmingham Barons, a minor-league baseball team. Though he wasn't as successful in baseball, it teaches us an important lesson about stepping out of our comfort zones and trying new things.

Humble Beginnings: Before his fame, Jordan grew up in a simple, working-class family, proving that it's not about where you come from, but where you're going that matters.

Nike Air Jordans: Jordan's signature shoe, the Air Jordan, created by Nike, has become a cultural icon. The sneakers' success demonstrates how sports can influence and transcend into fashion and culture. It shows that your influence can reach far beyond your primary profession.

Hall of Fame Speech: During his Hall of Fame speech in 2009, Jordan acknowledged everyone who doubted him throughout his career and thanked them for providing the motivation he needed to prove them wrong. This is a great reminder that sometimes, the people who doubt us can give us the motivation to work even harder.

Olympic Gold Medallist: Michael Jordan isn't just an NBA superstar; he's also an Olympic gold medalist. He won two gold medals with the U.S. men's basketball team in 1984 and 1992, reminding us to aim high and seek greatness on all stages.

Philanthropy: Jordan is a generous philanthropist. In 2020, he pledged to donate $100 million over ten years to organizations dedicated to ensuring racial equality. This teaches us the importance of giving back and using our success to make the world a better place.

Remember, every great achievement starts with a dream. So, dream big, work hard, and maybe one day, you could inspire others with your own story, just like Michael Jordan.

KOBE BRYANT

In Philadelphia, Pennsylvania, a young boy named Kobe Bryant fell in love with the game of basketball at the tender age of three. He was captivated by the sport, and he would spend countless hours practicing his skills. His passion for the game was clear even at such a young age.

Growing up, Kobe faced a significant challenge: his family moved to Italy when he was six years old. Suddenly, he found himself in a new country, having to learn a new language and adapt to a new culture. But even in this unfamiliar environment, one thing remained constant - his love for basketball.

In Italy, basketball wasn't as popular as in the United States. He didn't have the same resources or opportunities to develop his skills, but that didn't stop him. Kobe would practice with his father, who was a professional basketball player and learned from him. He would also watch NBA games on tapes and learn from his idols. Despite the circumstances, he made the most out of the situation.

Upon returning to the United States for high school, Kobe faced another challenge. He joined the varsity basketball team, and even though he had honed his skills in Italy, he struggled to adapt to the faster, more physical style of play in America. He didn't play much in his freshman year and even scored zero points in some games. For an aspiring player, this was a big setback.

However, Kobe didn't let this discourage him. He had a burning desire to be the best, and he was willing to put in the work necessary to achieve it. He would show up for practice hours before everyone else and stay hours afterward, honing his skills and improving his game. He turned his early struggles into motivation and worked incredibly hard to get better.

By his senior year, Kobe was recognized as the top high school basketball player in the country. He decided to skip college and enter the NBA draft directly, and he was selected by the Charlotte Hornets, who then traded him to the Los Angeles Lakers.

In the NBA, Kobe faced more challenges, but he always rose to the occasion. His work ethic, skill, and competitive spirit helped him become one of the greatest players in basketball history. He led the Lakers to five NBA championships, was named an All-Star 18 times, and even won an MVP award.

But perhaps the most inspiring part of Kobe's story is his mindset. He developed what he called the "Mamba Mentality," a mindset about loving the process of working hard and continually striving for improvement. He once said, "The most important thing is to try and inspire people so that they can be great in whatever they want to do."

Kobe's story teaches us that success is not just about talent; it's about hard work, resilience, and having the right mindset. His story reminds us that challenges and setbacks are not barriers to success, but opportunities for growth. No matter what your dream is, if you're willing to work for it and never give up, you can achieve it. That's the essence of the Mamba Mentality.

Fun Facts:

Multilingual: Kobe Bryant was fluent in several languages, including English, Italian, and Spanish. This demonstrates the importance of learning and expanding one's horizons beyond just their primary interest or skill.

Youngest Player: When Kobe entered the NBA in 1996, he was just 18 years old, making him the youngest player in NBA history at the time. This shows that age is not a barrier to achieving great things if you have the talent, determination, and work ethic.

High School to NBA: Kobe made the jump directly from high school to the NBA, which was quite rare at the time. He didn't let conventions or 'the usual path' restrict his dreams.

Named After a Steak: His parents named him Kobe after the famous beef of Kobe, Japan, which they saw on a restaurant menu. It's a quirky fact that adds a unique aspect to his persona.

Academy Award Winner: Kobe Bryant wasn't just a basketball player; he was also a storyteller. He won an Academy Award for Best Animated Short Film for "Dear Basketball" in 2018. This shows that we can have multiple talents and passions and we shouldn't be afraid to explore them.

The Black Mamba: Kobe gave himself the nickname "Black Mamba," inspired by the agile and deadly snake, as a way to separate his professional life from his personal life. It's a lesson about developing a strong mindset and the importance of balance in life.

Books for Young Readers: Kobe also started a series of books for young readers called "The Wizenard Series". The series focuses on magic, sports, and the power of self-belief. It's a testament to his passion for inspiring and teaching younger generations.

Loving Father: Kobe was a dedicated and loving father to his four daughters. He was known for his active involvement in their lives and always encouraged them to chase their dreams.

These facts about Kobe Bryant show us that he was more than just a basketball player. He was a multifaceted person who used his fame and talent to inspire and influence people around the world. His life teaches us the value of hard work, resilience, and exploring our passions, and that success can come in many forms beyond what we initially envision.

SHAQUILLE O'NEAL

Some time ago, in the busy city of Newark, New Jersey, a little boy named Shaquille Rashaun O'Neal was born. Shaq's biological father was not present in his life, and his mother, Lucille O'Neal, struggled to make ends meet. However, the challenges didn't stop Lucille from instilling strong values and a sense of determination in her son.

When Shaq was just a toddler, Lucille married Sergeant Phillip Harrison, who became Shaq's stepfather. Despite the hardships of living in a neighborhood riddled with crime, Shaq found solace in basketball and looked up to his stepfather, who was strict but supportive.

Shaq was always the biggest kid in his class. This made him stand out and sometimes made him feel awkward. But instead of letting it get to him, he used his height to his advantage on the basketball court.

Despite his obvious talent and size, Shaq struggled with his shooting. He couldn't make free throws to save his life, and this became a point of frustration for him. Instead of giving up, he kept practicing. He'd spend hours after school shooting free throws, trying to improve.

His efforts paid off. He led his high school team to a state championship and earned a scholarship to Louisiana State University. In college, he was a standout player, and after three years, he declared for the NBA Draft.

Shaq was the first overall pick in the 1992 NBA Draft, selected by the Orlando Magic. His rookie season was phenomenal, and he was named the Rookie of the Year. He was already making a name for himself in the NBA, but he still had a lot to prove.

His free-throw shooting, which he had worked so hard on, was still a weak point. Critics said he would never be a great player because of it. But Shaq didn't let the criticism deter him. He continued to work hard, and his perseverance began to show results.

Shaq led the Los Angeles Lakers to three consecutive championships from 2000 to 2002, and later helped the Miami Heat win a championship in 2006. His dynamic personality, combined with his basketball skills, made him one of the most popular players in the NBA.

One of the most inspiring things about Shaq is his humble nature and his desire to give back. He has said, "My mother and father always taught me that if you have a little, try to help others. If you have a lot, you must do a lot more." Over the years, he's been involved in various charitable activities, showing his big heart matches his stature.

Shaq's story teaches us that no matter where we come from, we can rise above our circumstances. His dedication to his craft, despite his struggles, shows us the importance of hard work and perseverance. And his generosity reminds us that success is not just about what we achieve for ourselves, but also about how we use our success to help others.

Fun Facts:

Nickname: Shaq has many nicknames, including "The Diesel", "Superman", and "The Big Aristotle". These nicknames show his playful personality and how he brings joy to everything he does.

Education: Even after becoming a successful NBA player, Shaq understood the value of education. He went back to school and earned his bachelor's degree, a master's degree in business administration, and even a doctorate in education. This demonstrates that learning doesn't stop once school is over, and that education is valuable at any age.

Musical Talent: Shaq is not only a talented basketball player, but he's also musically inclined. He has released several rap albums, one of which ("Shaq Diesel") even went platinum. This shows that we can have more than one talent and we should explore our interests to the fullest.

Acting Career: Shaq has appeared in movies and TV shows, including "Blue Chips", "Kazaam", and "Shaq Vs." His varied career shows that we can always try new things and not be confined to just one path.

Law Enforcement: Shaq has a deep respect for law enforcement and has become a reserve officer for various police departments across the United States. He shows that we can make a difference in our communities in many different ways.

Sports Analyst: After retiring from professional basketball, Shaq became an analyst on the television program Inside the NBA. His successful transition shows that we can reinvent ourselves and adapt to new roles throughout our lives.

Generosity: Shaq is known for his generous spirit. He often gives back to his community, whether it's buying shoes for a young boy with large feet or donating to various charities. This teaches us the importance of helping others and using our success to make a difference.

NBA Records: Shaq holds numerous NBA records and has received many accolades, including being named one of the 50 Greatest Players in NBA History. His achievements are a testament to his hard work and dedication to his sport.

Basketball Rim Tree: Shaq was known for breaking multiple basketball rims and with his humorous nature he made a basket rim tree from all the rims he broke throughout his career.

Remember, just like Shaq, never limit yourself to just one thing. Explore all of your interests, always strive for education, work hard, and don't forget to give back. That's the recipe for a truly successful and fulfilling life.

LEBRON JAMES

LeBron James was born in Akron, Ohio, in 1984. His mother, Gloria James, was only 16 years old at the time. She raised him alone because LeBron's father wasn't in the picture. They didn't have much and often moved from one apartment to another, making it hard for LeBron to make friends and have a normal childhood.

Despite these challenges, LeBron found comfort in sports. He excelled in basketball and football and was recognized for his exceptional athleticism even at a young age.

When LeBron was in fourth grade, his life took a significant turn. He missed almost 100 days of school because his family didn't have a stable home. A local football coach, Frank Walker, learned about LeBron's situation and took him in. He introduced LeBron to basketball and even bought him his first pair of basketball shoes.

Having a stable home helped LeBron thrive. He began to excel academically and athletically. His natural talent combined with hard work quickly made him a basketball prodigy. By the time he was in eighth grade, he was already being scouted by college basketball programs.

LeBron attended St. Vincent-St. Mary High School, where he and his friends, Sian Cotton, Dru Joyce III, and Willie McGee, became the core of one of the best high school basketball teams in the country. Despite the attention and pressure, LeBron remained focused on his game and his studies.

In his senior year, LeBron was undoubtedly the best high school basketball player in the country. Instead of going to college, he declared for the NBA draft. He was picked first overall by the Cleveland Cavaliers and quickly rose to stardom. He has since won four NBA championships, four MVP awards, and two Olympic gold medals.

But what's truly inspiring about LeBron isn't just his success on the court; it's how he's used that success to give back to his community. In 2018, he opened the "I PROMISE School" in his hometown of Akron, a public school aimed at helping at-risk children get a high-quality education. The school provides free tuition, uniforms, bicycles, and helmets, free breakfast, lunch, and snacks, and guaranteed tuition for all graduates of the University of Akron.

LeBron's story teaches us that no matter how tough our circumstances may be, we can rise above them with determination, hard work, and a little help from caring individuals. His dedication to giving back to his community shows us that success is not just about personal achievements, but also about lifting others up and making a positive impact on the world.

Fun Facts:

Young Prodigy: LeBron James was so good at basketball that he was featured on the cover of "Sports Illustrated" when he was just a high school junior, with the magazine dubbing him "The Chosen One".

Straight to NBA: LeBron was selected with the first overall pick in the 2003 NBA Draft by the Cleveland Cavaliers straight out of high school, becoming one of the few players to make such a leap.

Multi-sport Athlete: LeBron was an excellent football player in high school, and some believe he could have played in the NFL. This shows that he was not only talented in basketball but also versatile in his athletic abilities.

Philanthropy: LeBron launched the LeBron James Family Foundation, which spends millions of dollars on programs like providing a guaranteed four-year college scholarship to the University of Akron to all eligible students who graduate from his "I PROMISE School" and complete community service requirements.

Education Commitment: LeBron established the "I PROMISE School" in his hometown of Akron, Ohio. This public school is designed to help underprivileged children succeed, demonstrating LeBron's commitment to giving back to his community.

Film and TV: LeBron is also a film and television producer. He has produced and appeared in several films and TV shows, proving that it's possible to have diverse interests and achievements.

Healthy Living: LeBron is known for taking exceptional care of his body. He has a rigorous exercise routine, follows a healthy diet, and values rest and recovery time. This highlights the importance of maintaining good health in order to perform at your best.

Love for Reading: LeBron is an avid reader and is often spotted reading books before games. He believes reading helps him calm his mind and focus, showing kids the power of a good book.

Loyalty: Despite receiving offers from several prestigious teams, LeBron decided to return to his home team, the Cleveland Cavaliers, in 2014 after a stint with Miami Heat. He wanted to give back to his hometown and fulfilled his promise by leading the Cavaliers to their first-ever NBA championship in 2016.

Records: LeBron holds multiple NBA records including an all-time scoring record passing Kareem Abdul-Jabbar and is the only player in the history of the NBA to record at least 30,000 points, 10,000 rebounds, and 10,000 assists

These facts about LeBron James show that he is more than just an exceptional athlete. He is also a philanthropist, a committed student of life, and a person who values his health and community. His story inspires kids to dream big, work hard, and never forget the importance of giving back to their communities.

CHARLES BARKLEY

Charles Wade Barkley was born and raised in a small town in Alabama. He grew up in a modest, working-class family. His father left when he was a baby, leaving his mother and grandmother to raise him and his two brothers.

Growing up, Barkley was a chubby kid who loved basketball. However, he didn't make his high school varsity team until he was a senior. This was because he stood at only 5'10", relatively short for the game he loved. This setback, however, didn't deter Charles from pursuing his passion.

In his senior year of high school, Charles experienced a significant growth spurt, which saw him grow to 6'4". His game drastically improved and he led his high school team to the state semifinals. His performance caught the attention of Auburn University, where he got a scholarship to play basketball.

At Auburn, Barkley continued to face challenges due to his size. He was shorter than most power forwards and he struggled to keep his weight under control. But he used these perceived disadvantages to his benefit. His unique combination of power and agility, along with an uncanny ability to rebound, earned him the nickname "The Round Mound of Rebound."

Barkley entered the NBA draft after his junior year and was picked by the Philadelphia 76ers. In the NBA, Barkley stood out not just because of his unconventional size for a power forward, but also for his tenacity, energy, and sheer talent. He went on to have an exceptional career, including an MVP season in 1993 and 11 All-Star appearances.

But beyond his accomplishments on the court, Charles Barkley is known for his personality and his honesty. He's never shied away from speaking his mind, even when his opinions were unpopular. He's used his platform to bring attention to social issues and has been involved in various charitable activities.

Barkley's journey teaches us that physical characteristics don't define our potential. He faced a lot of challenges, but he used them to fuel his determination and pave his own path. His story also shows the importance of speaking up for what we believe in and using our success to make a difference in the world.

Fun Facts:

Overcoming Obstacles: Despite not being as tall as most of his peers, Barkley used his strength and speed to outperform many of his opponents. He was often called "The Round Mound of Rebound" due to his shape and exceptional ability to rebound the ball.

Exceptional Career: Charles Barkley had an outstanding career in the NBA. He was an 11-time All-Star, a league Most Valuable Player (MVP) in 1993, and he is now a member of the Basketball Hall of Fame.

Olympian: Barkley was a key player on the Dream Team, the 1992 USA Olympic Basketball team that is often considered the greatest basketball team ever assembled. He was the leading scorer of the team and helped the USA win a gold medal.

Education Matters: Despite leaving Auburn University early to join the NBA, Barkley later returned to complete his degree. This shows the importance he places on education.

TV Personality: After retiring from basketball, Barkley became an analyst on the show "Inside the NBA." His candid, humorous, and sometimes controversial commentary has earned him several sports Emmy Awards.

Social Activism: Barkley is known for speaking his mind and has used his platform to advocate for social justice. He's also involved in various charitable activities, showing his dedication to giving back to the community.

Author: Barkley has written several books, sharing his opinions and experiences on a range of topics. This shows his commitment to sharing his knowledge and experiences to inspire others.

Nicknames: Apart from "The Round Mound of Rebound," Barkley was also known as "Sir Charles." His nicknames are part of his unique and charismatic personality that's loved by fans worldwide.

These facts about Charles Barkley show us that regardless of physical characteristics, we can excel if we are determined and work hard. Barkley's story also tells us that education is important, it's necessary to voice our opinions, and it's our duty to give back to our community.

Magic Johnson

Earvin "Magic" Johnson Jr. was born in Lansing, Michigan, in 1959. He was the seventh of ten children in his family. His father worked on the assembly line at General Motors while his mother was a school custodian. Johnson often helped his father on his trash hauling service, which taught him about hard work from a young age.

Johnson's love for basketball started early, and by the time he was in high school, he was already a dominant player. He earned his nickname "Magic" from a sports writer who had just watched the 15-year-old Johnson record a triple-double (points, rebounds, and assists) in a high school game.

After a successful high school career, Johnson attended Michigan State University. In 1979, he led the team to the NCAA championship victory over Larry Bird's Indiana State, setting the stage for one of the greatest rivalries in basketball history.

Johnson entered the NBA in 1979 when he was selected first overall by the Los Angeles Lakers. In his rookie season, he led the Lakers to a championship and was named the NBA Finals MVP. Johnson's career was marked by numerous accolades, including five NBA championships, three MVP awards, and 12 All-Star appearances.

However, in 1991, Johnson faced his greatest challenge. He announced that he had tested positive for HIV, a virus that was, at that time, often seen as a death sentence and associated with significant stigma. Johnson's announcement shocked the world, but he faced his diagnosis with courage and determination. He used his platform to raise awareness about HIV/AIDS and became a spokesperson.

Despite retiring from professional basketball, Johnson wasn't done with the NBA. He became part-owner of the Lakers and later took on a role as the team's president of basketball operations. Outside of basketball, he's a successful businessman, owning a chain of movie theaters, and he's also involved in real estate and other business ventures.

More importantly, Magic Johnson has dedicated his life to philanthropy. His Magic Johnson Foundation provides funds for HIV/AIDS research, scholarships for financially disadvantaged students, and community empowerment centers in underserved neighborhoods.

Magic Johnson's story is a powerful example of resilience, courage, and the will to make a positive change. He shows us that no matter what challenges we face, we can use them as opportunities to grow and to help others. Even after achieving success, we should remember to give back to our community and use our platform to make a difference.

Fun Facts:

Nickname Origin: Magic Johnson's real name is Earvin Johnson Jr. He got his nickname "Magic" when he was in high school because of his amazing skills on the basketball court. A sports writer coined the nickname after witnessing a young Johnson score a triple-double.

Impressive Rookie Season: In his rookie season with the Lakers, Johnson led the team to win the NBA Championship. He played as a center in place of the injured Kareem Abdul-Jabbar in Game 6 of the NBA Finals and recorded 42 points, 15 rebounds, and 7 assists. He remains the only rookie to win the NBA Finals MVP award.

Versatile Player: Magic was known for his versatility on the court. Although he was a point guard, he could play and defend multiple positions. His extraordinary vision and passing skills changed the way the point guard position was played.

Olympic Gold Medalist: Magic was a member of the original "Dream Team," the U.S. basketball team for the 1992 Olympics. The team, which many consider the greatest basketball team ever assembled, easily won the gold medal.

Successful Businessman: After retiring from basketball, Magic became a successful entrepreneur. He has owned movie theaters and gyms, and he's part of the group that owns the Los Angeles Dodgers and the Los Angeles Sparks.

HIV/AIDS Advocate: Since his HIV diagnosis in 1991, Magic has been a strong advocate for HIV/AIDS awareness. He's used his platform to promote safe contact and reduce the stigma associated with HIV/AIDS.

Philanthropy: Magic established the Magic Johnson Foundation to support HIV/AIDS research, provide scholarships, and help communities in need. This shows his commitment to making a difference in people's lives off the court.

Love for Family: Magic is known for his love and commitment to his family. He's been married to his wife, Cookie, since 1991, and they have a son named EJ.

Magic Johnson's story shows that success is not only about our achievements but also about how we use those achievements to make a positive impact on the world. His career is an example of determination, versatility, and the importance of caring for others.

David Robinson

David Maurice Robinson, often known as "The Admiral," was born in Key West, Florida, in 1965. His father was a U.S. Navy officer, which led the family to move several times during Robinson's childhood.

Robinson's passion for basketball developed in his middle school years. By the time he entered high school, he was an impressive player. However, he prioritized his academics and planned to study mathematics or engineering in college. His basketball prowess grew parallel to his academic success, earning him a place at the U.S. Naval Academy.

Although his intent was to focus on his studies, Robinson's skills on the basketball court didn't go unnoticed. Over the course of his college career, he grew from 6'8" to 7'1". His growth spurt, coupled with his athletic prowess, made him a force to be reckoned with in collegiate basketball. Robinson led the Navy Midshipmen to several successful seasons and won numerous awards, including the prestigious Naismith and Wooden Awards.

When Robinson graduated, he was drafted first overall by the San Antonio Spurs in the 1987 NBA draft. However, he had to fulfill his service commitment to the Navy, so he didn't start playing professionally until two years later. He took his commitment seriously and served as a civil engineering officer at the Naval Submarine Base Kings Bay in Georgia.

Robinson eventually started his NBA career in 1989. He quickly established himself as one of the top centers in the league and led the Spurs to the greatest single-season turnaround in NBA history at the time. He won Rookie of the Year and, later in his career, earned two NBA championships, an MVP award, and 10 All-Star appearances. Robinson is also one of the few players to score over 70 points in a single NBA game.

Off the court, Robinson is known for his philanthropy. In 2001, he founded the Carver Academy in San Antonio, a non-profit college preparatory school to help students from underserved communities. He donated $5 million of his own money to start the school and has since donated millions more.

David Robinson's story is inspiring in many ways. He shows us the importance of education and honoring our commitments. He proves that with dedication, we can excel in many areas, whether it's basketball, mathematics, or serving our country. Robinson's philanthropy also demonstrates that giving back to the community is an essential part of success.

Fun Facts:

Academic Excellence: David Robinson was a very good student. He scored 1320 on his SAT and was very focused on his academics, which led him to attend the U.S. Naval Academy.

Service Commitment: After being drafted first overall by the San Antonio Spurs in the 1987 NBA draft, Robinson didn't immediately start his professional basketball career. He honored his service commitment to the Navy first, showing his dedication and loyalty.

Impressive Growth Spurt: Robinson was already an impressive 6'8" when he entered college, but over the course of his time at the U.S. Naval Academy, he grew to an incredible height of 7'1".

Outstanding Player: Robinson is one of the greatest centers in the history of the NBA. He was a 10-time All-Star, won two NBA championships, and was the league's MVP in 1995. He's one of the few players to score over 70 points in a single game.

Olympic Gold Medalist: Robinson is a two-time Olympic Gold Medalist, winning in 1992 and 1996 with the U.S. men's basketball team.

Hall of Famer: Robinson was inducted into the Naismith Memorial Basketball Hall of Fame twice – once for his individual career in 2009 and again in 2010 as a member of the "Dream Team," the 1992 Olympic basketball team.

Philanthropist: Off the court, Robinson is known for his philanthropy. He established the Carver Academy, a non-profit college preparatory school in San Antonio, to which he donated $5 million of his own money.

Successful Businessman: After retiring from basketball, Robinson went on to become a successful businessman. He co-founded Admiral Capital Group, a private equity firm.

Musical Talent: In addition to his other talents, Robinson also plays the piano and saxophone.

David Robinson's life shows us that we can excel in many areas if we put in the effort. Whether it's academics, sports, music, or serving our community, we can make a positive impact in many ways. His story is an example of dedication, loyalty, and the importance of giving back.

Kareem Abdul-Jabbar

Born Ferdinand Lewis Alcindor Jr. on April 16, 1947, in New York City, Kareem was the only child of his parents. From an early age, it was clear that he was going to be tall. By the time he was in 8th grade, he had already reached 6'8", taller than most adults.

Kareem started playing basketball at a young age and attended Power Memorial Academy, a Catholic high school in Manhattan. There, he led his team to three straight New York City Catholic championships, a 71-game winning streak, and a 79–2 overall record, making the team one of the best high school basketball teams in New York City history.

He then went on to play for UCLA in college, where he was coached by the legendary John Wooden. His college career was nothing short of brilliant: his team won three consecutive NCAA championships, and he was recognized as the tournament's Most Outstanding Player each time.

When Kareem entered the NBA as the number one draft pick in 1969, he quickly made an impact. His "skyhook" shot became his trademark and is still considered one of the most effective shots in the history of basketball. Kareem played twenty seasons in the NBA for the Milwaukee Bucks and the Los Angeles Lakers, winning six NBA championships and six Most Valuable Player (MVP) awards.

In 1971, Kareem converted to Islam and changed his name from Ferdinand Lewis Alcindor Jr. to Kareem Abdul-Jabbar, which means "noble, powerful servant."

In 1985, he broke the NBA all-time scoring record, previously held by Wilt Chamberlain, which has now been broken by Lebron James. He retired in 1989 at the age of 42.

However, his impact goes beyond basketball. Abdul-Jabbar has been an activist for social justice throughout his life. He has written numerous books and articles on the subject and has used his platform to advocate for change.

In 2016, Abdul-Jabbar was awarded the Presidential Medal of Freedom, the highest civilian award of the United States, by President Barack Obama.

Kareem Abdul-Jabbar's story is one of dedication, hard work, and resilience. His journey teaches us the value of mastering our unique skills (like his skyhook shot), standing up for what we believe in, and striving for excellence in all that we do. His accomplishments on and off the court make him an inspiring figure for children and adults alike.

Fun Facts:

Skyhook Shot: Kareem is renowned for his "skyhook" shot, which he used to score many of his record-setting points. This unique shot, which he mastered, is still considered one of the most effective and hardest-to-block shots in basketball.

Record-Breaker: Kareem held the record for the most points scored in NBA history, with a staggering 38,387 points over his career. Which has recently been broken bt Lebron James

Champion: Over his 20-year professional career with the Milwaukee Bucks and Los Angeles Lakers, Abdul-Jabbar won six NBA championships and was selected as an All-Star 19 times.

Name Change: Kareem was born as Ferdinand Lewis Alcindor Jr. but changed his name to Kareem Abdul-Jabbar after converting to Islam in 1971. His chosen name translates to "noble, powerful servant."

Author and Activist: Kareem is not only a basketball player but also an author and an activist. He has written several books, including memoirs, history books, and children's books. He is known for speaking out on social and political issues.

Award Winner: In 2016, Kareem was awarded the Presidential Medal of Freedom, the highest civilian honor in the United States, by President Barack Obama.

Film and Television Appearances: Abdul-Jabbar has had several appearances in film and TV. He famously co-starred in the 1980 comedy film "Airplane!" and has made appearances on shows like "Full House" and "The Big Bang Theory."

Loves Jazz Music: Kareem is a huge jazz fan. He even co-produced a documentary called "On the Shoulders of Giants," which celebrates the Harlem Rens, a basketball team of the 1920s and '30s, and their influence on the Harlem Renaissance.

Kareem Abdul-Jabbar's life and career show that it's possible to succeed in many different areas, not just in sports. His dedication to mastering his craft, his commitment to his beliefs, and his desire to use his platform for

positive change can inspire kids to strive for their best in whatever they
choose to do.

KEVIN DURANT

Kevin Wayne Durant was born on September 29, 1988, in Washington, D.C. He was raised by his mother, Wanda Durant, along with his brother, sister, and grandmother. Durant fell in love with basketball at a young age. He was tall for his age and by the time he reached high school, he was already 6'3".

As a teenager, Durant faced many challenges. He grew up in a neighborhood plagued by crime and poverty. However, Durant's mother was a powerful influence in his life, working hard to keep her children on the right path. In fact, Durant often refers to his mother as "The Real MVP" for her unwavering support and sacrifice.

In high school, Durant became a star player and was heavily recruited by top college basketball programs. He eventually chose to attend the University of Texas, where he played for just one year but made a significant impact, winning numerous awards including the prestigious Wooden Award.

Durant declared for the NBA draft after his freshman year of college and was selected by the Seattle SuperSonics with the second overall pick. He quickly established himself as a top player in the NBA, winning Rookie of the Year in his first season.

Over the years, Durant became known for his scoring ability, ball-handling skills, and versatility on the court. He won several NBA scoring titles, an MVP award, and two NBA Championships with the Golden State Warriors. However, Durant's journey was not always smooth. He faced injuries and had to overcome significant setbacks, including a ruptured Achilles tendon during the 2019 NBA Finals.

Off the court, Durant is known for his philanthropy. In 2013, he donated $1 million to the Red Cross for tornado relief efforts in Oklahoma. In 2018, he committed $10 million to the College Track program, which aims to help disadvantaged students attend and graduate from college.

Kevin Durant's journey is an inspiring example of overcoming adversity, pursuing a dream, and achieving success while staying grounded and giving back to the community. His hard work, perseverance, and generosity can serve as motivation for kids everywhere.

Fun Facts:

High School Star: Durant was so good at basketball in high school that he was named the Washington Post All-Met Basketball Player of the Year.

College Success: Despite playing only one year of college basketball at the University of Texas, Durant won the John R. Wooden Award given to the country's best player.

NBA Star: Durant was the NBA Rookie of the Year in 2008 and has been an NBA All-Star multiple times. He has won multiple NBA Championships and was named the NBA Finals MVP in 2017 and 2018.

Olympic Gold Medalist: Durant has represented the USA in the Olympics and has won multiple gold medals.

Record Breaker: Durant is the youngest player in NBA history to win a scoring title, which he won in the 2009-2010 season when he was just 21.

Philanthropy: Durant has a big heart. After a tornado devastated parts of Oklahoma, where he played for the Oklahoma City Thunder, he donated $1 million to the Red Cross to help the recovery efforts. He also committed $10 million to the College Track program, which helps disadvantaged students attend college.

Resilience: Durant suffered a serious Achilles tendon injury during the 2019 NBA Finals but made an impressive comeback, proving his incredible determination and resilience.

Nickname: Durant's fans often refer to him as "KD" or "Durantula," a nickname that combines his last name with tarantula, due to his impressive wingspan on the court.

Love for Photography: Off the court, Durant is a passionate photographer. He even served as a credentialed photographer at the Super Bowl in 2016.

Kevin Durant's story and achievements highlight the power of dedication, resilience, and generosity, and serve as great inspiration for kids, showing them that they can achieve their dreams with hard work and perseverance, and that it's always important to give back to their communities.

Stephen Curry

Stephen Curry was born on March 14, 1988, in Akron, Ohio. He grew up in a sports-oriented family. His father, Dell Curry, was a professional NBA player, and his mother, Sonya, was a standout volleyball player in college.

Despite his family's athletic history, Curry's journey to NBA stardom wasn't straightforward. As a teenager, he was overlooked by many college scouts due to his small stature and lean frame. Despite his skill, he didn't receive any scholarship offers from major college basketball programs.

Instead of being discouraged, Curry chose to attend Davidson College, a small school in North Carolina, where he received an opportunity to play. It was there that Curry began to shine, leading the nation in scoring and becoming a consensus first-team All-American during his sophomore and junior years.

Despite his success in college, many doubted Curry's ability to succeed in the NBA due to his size and perceived lack of strength. However, he was selected as the 7th overall pick by the Golden State Warriors in the 2009 NBA Draft, and he proved his doubters wrong.

In the NBA, Curry became known for
his incredible shooting ability, especially
from the three-point range. He redefined
the game with his deep shooting,
including regularly making shots from
well beyond the three-point line. His
excellent skills and unique style of
play helped him lead the Golden State
Warriors to several NBA championships.

Off the court, Curry is known for his
charity work. He's involved in numerous philanthropic efforts, including
Nothing But Nets, an initiative that delivers bed nets to communities in
Africa to fight malaria.

Stephen Curry's story is inspiring because it shows that size and strength
aren't the only measures of success in sports. His journey also teaches kids
the importance of perseverance, hard work, and the willingness to pave
your own path, even when others doubt you. Curry's passion for the game,
his humility, and his dedication to giving back to the community make him
a great role model for children.

Fun Facts:

Underdog Story: Despite his undeniable talent, Curry was not heavily recruited out of high school. He ended up at Davidson College, a small school, and used this as motivation to work even harder.

NBA Records: Curry holds the record for the most three-pointers made in a single season. He set this record during the 2015-2016 NBA season when he made an astonishing 402 three-pointers.

Family of Athletes: Both his father, Dell Curry, and his brother, Seth Curry, have played in the NBA. His mother, Sonya, was a standout volleyball player. Sports run deep in the Curry family!

MVP Awards: Curry has won multiple NBA Most Valuable Player (MVP) awards, including becoming the first player in history to be voted MVP by a unanimous decision in 2016.

Charity Work: Curry is known for his charity work, specifically with the United Nations Foundation's Nothing But Nets campaign, which delivers bed nets to help families in Africa prevent malaria.

Golf Enthusiast: When he's not shooting hoops, Curry loves to play golf. He's quite good at it, too! He's even competed in professional golf tournaments.

Love for Popcorn: Curry has a well-known love for popcorn. He rates the popcorn at every NBA arena and has been known to have popcorn as a pregame snack.

Animated Character: Curry has appeared as an animated version of himself in the popular cartoon show, "Family Guy."

Owns a Production Company: Off the court, Curry owns a production company called Unanimous Media, which produces film and television projects focusing on faith, family, and sports themes.

Stephen Curry's story inspires kids to work hard, make the most of opportunities, and use their success to help others. He also shows that having a balanced life with different interests (like his love for golf and his production company) can enrich your main passion. His achievements and character make him a great role model for children.

STEVE NASH

Born in Johannesburg, South Africa, in 1974, Nash moved to Canada when he was just 18 months old. His athletic talent was apparent from a young age, but his first love was soccer, not basketball. He played ice hockey, soccer, and rugby in his childhood and early teens before turning to basketball.

Despite his talent, Nash was overlooked by many college scouts and did not receive any significant scholarship offers from U.S. colleges. Eventually, he received a scholarship to Santa Clara University, a small school in California. Nash excelled at Santa Clara, leading the team to three NCAA tournament appearances and making a name for himself as a standout player.

In 1996, Nash was drafted by the Phoenix Suns in the NBA Draft. His first two seasons were a struggle, and he was even traded to the Dallas Mavericks. However, Nash used these setbacks as motivation to improve his game. He developed into one of the best point guards in the NBA, earning a reputation for his playmaking, shooting, and leadership.

After several successful seasons with the Mavericks, Nash returned to the Suns, where he won back-to-back Most Valuable Player (MVP) awards in 2005 and 2006, becoming one of the few players in history to achieve this feat.

Despite his individual success, Nash was also known for his unselfish play and dedication to his teammates. He consistently ranked among the league leaders in assists and is widely regarded as one of the greatest passers in NBA history.

Off the court, Nash has been heavily involved in philanthropy. He founded the Steve Nash Foundation in 2001, which aims to assist underserved children in their health, personal development, education, and enjoyment of life.

Steve Nash's story is one of resilience, hard work, and the drive to constantly improve. It teaches you, kids, that setbacks and challenges can be used as motivation to achieve your goals. It also shows the importance of teamwork and using your success to help others, both important lessons for children.

Fun Facts:

Multi-sport Athlete: Before focusing on basketball, Nash played soccer, ice hockey, and rugby. He still loves soccer and has even been part of the ownership group for the Vancouver Whitecaps of Major League Soccer.

Back-to-Back MVP: Nash won back-to-back NBA Most Valuable Player (MVP) awards in 2005 and 2006, joining an elite group of players to have accomplished this feat.

Canadian Pride: Nash is one of the most successful Canadian basketball players of all time. In 2007, he was awarded the Order of Canada, the highest civilian honor in the country.

Charitable Efforts: Nash established the Steve Nash Foundation in 2001, which is dedicated to helping underprivileged children around the world.

Film Lover: Nash is a big fan of film and has even dabbled in film-making. He co-directed "Into the Wind," a documentary about Canadian runner Terry Fox, which aired as part of ESPN's 30 for 30 series.

Hall of Famer: In recognition of his incredible career, Nash was inducted into the Naismith Memorial Basketball Hall of Fame in 2018.

NBA Coach: After his playing career, Nash became a coach. He was named head coach of the Brooklyn Nets in 2020.

Fitness Enthusiast: Even after retirement, Nash has stayed in excellent shape. He's known for his commitment to fitness and healthy living.

Sustainable Living Advocate: Nash is a big advocate for sustainable living. He drives a hybrid vehicle and has often spoken about the importance of combating climate change.

Steve Nash's story is a testament to perseverance, passion, and the power of hard work. His achievements on and off the court can inspire kids to pursue their passions, work hard, and use their success to make a positive impact in their communities.

LARRY BIRD

Larry Bird was born on December 7, 1956, in the small town of French Lick, Indiana. He came from a poor family and lived in a house that didn't even have indoor plumbing. Bird's family struggled to make ends meet, but he found comfort in the game of basketball.

Despite his family's financial difficulties, Bird developed a strong work ethic, often practicing basketball for hours on end. He led his high school basketball team to the state finals and later played at Indiana State University, leading them to the NCAA finals.

Bird entered the NBA in 1979 when he was selected by the Boston Celtics. Even in a team filled with legends, Bird stood out. His work ethic, combined with his natural talent, made him one of the greatest players in the history of the sport.

Bird, known as "Larry Legend," became a 12-time NBA All-Star and three-time Most Valuable Player (MVP). He led the Celtics to three NBA Championships and was later named to the NBA's 50th Anniversary All-Time Team.

Despite his incredible success, Bird never forgot where he came from. He was known for his humility and credited his success to his relentless work ethic and dedication to the game.

After retiring from playing, Bird served as a coach and an executive in the NBA, proving that there's always a way to stay connected to your passion. As the President of Basketball Operations for the Indiana Pacers, Bird was named NBA Executive of the Year in 2012, making him the only person in NBA history to win MVP, Coach of the Year, and Executive of the Year.

Larry Bird's story teaches kids that no matter where you come from, with hard work, dedication, and a love for what you do, you can achieve great things. His story also highlights the importance of humility and remembering your roots, no matter how successful you become.

Fun Facts:

Humble Beginnings: Bird grew up in a small town, French Lick, Indiana, which led to his nickname "The Hick from French Lick."

Multi-sport Athlete: Bird was not only a fantastic basketball player but also played baseball in high school and was good enough to be drafted by the Cincinnati Reds. However, he didn't sign with the team and instead focused on basketball.

Triple-Double Machine: Bird was known for his versatility on the court. He is one of the NBA players with the most triple-doubles in his career.

Clutch Performer: Bird had a reputation for performing his best in high-pressure situations. His clutch shooting in the final moments of games was a major part of his legend.

Coaching and Executive Success: After his playing career, Bird served as a coach and an executive in the NBA. He was named NBA Executive of the Year in 2012, making him the only person in NBA history to win MVP, Coach of the Year, and Executive of the Year.

50-40-90 Club: Bird is one of the few players in NBA history to have joined the 50-40-90 club (50% field goal, 40% three-point, 90% free throw shooting in a single season), which is a testament to his incredible shooting efficiency.

Trash Talking Legend: Bird was known for his ability to get into his opponents' heads with his trash talk. But it was all in good fun and part of the competitive spirit of the game.

Dedication to Practice: Bird was known for his incredible work ethic. He would often arrive hours before games to practice his shooting.

Rivalry with Magic: Bird's rivalry with Magic Johnson, which started in college when Bird's Indiana State played Johnson's Michigan State in the NCAA championship, is one of the most famous in basketball history. Despite their fierce competition on the court, they became good friends off it.

Larry Bird's story can inspire kids to work hard, stay dedicated, and pursue their passion, no matter where they come from. His success also shows that even at the top, it's important to keep working to improve, maintain a competitive spirit, and most importantly, enjoy the game.

TIM DUNCAN

Born and raised in the U.S. Virgin Islands, Tim Duncan's first love was not basketball, but swimming. He was one of the top competitive swimmers in his age group and had dreams of becoming an Olympian. However, his plans changed when Hurricane Hugo destroyed the only Olympic-sized swimming pool on the island in 1989. Tim became afraid of swimming in the ocean, so he turned to basketball, a sport he previously only played casually.

In high school, he quickly drew attention to his skill and was recruited to play for Wake Forest University. During his four years at Wake Forest, he won numerous awards and was recognized as one of the top college players in the nation.

Duncan was drafted by the San Antonio Spurs with the first overall pick in the 1997 NBA Draft. He would spend his entire 19-year career with the Spurs, demonstrating an unmatched level of loyalty and consistency. Together with Coach Gregg Popovich, Duncan led the Spurs to five NBA Championships and was named the Finals MVP three times.

Despite his fame and success, Duncan was known for his quiet demeanor and humble personality. He didn't seek out the spotlight and instead, let his performance on the court speak for itself. His consistent and fundamental style of play earned him the nickname "The Big Fundamental."

Off the court, Duncan is an avid fan of role-playing games and has a love for cars and auto racing. He also established the Tim Duncan Foundation, which has raised millions of dollars for health awareness and research, education, and youth sports in various communities.

After retiring from basketball, Duncan joined the Spurs' coaching staff, continuing his commitment to the team and sport he loves.

Tim Duncan's story is an example of how unexpected changes can lead to new opportunities. His humble demeanor, combined with his consistent performance and dedication to the game, can inspire kids to stay grounded, work hard, and remain adaptable in the face of change.

Fun Facts:

Island Roots: Duncan grew up in the U.S. Virgin Islands and was originally a competitive swimmer before he started playing basketball.

Academic All-American: Duncan was not only a star on the court in college but also in the classroom. He was named an Academic All-American during his time at Wake Forest University.

Consistency: Duncan spent his entire 19-year career with the San Antonio Spurs, which is a rare feat in the modern NBA. During that time, the Spurs never missed the playoffs.

Impressive Records: He's one of the few players in NBA history to reach over 26,000 points, 15,000 rebounds, and 3,000 blocked shots in his career.

Nickname: Duncan was often referred to as "The Big Fundamental" because of his focus on fundamental basketball skills.

Philanthropy: He established the Tim Duncan Foundation, which supports health awareness, education, and youth sports in various communities.

Love for Games: Duncan is known for his love of Dungeons & Dragons and video games, proving that you can be a star athlete and a "nerd" at the same time.

Car Enthusiast: Duncan is a big fan of cars and even owns a car customization shop in San Antonio.

Coach Duncan: After retiring from professional basketball, Duncan joined the San Antonio Spurs coaching staff, showing his continued dedication to the sport and the team.

Tim Duncan's story illustrates the importance of adaptability, dedication, consistency, and humility. His love for learning, whether it's mastering basketball fundamentals or enjoying role-playing games, can inspire kids to follow their passions and never stop learning.

ALLEN IVERSON

Born in Hampton, Virginia, Iverson came from a challenging background. He grew up in poverty, often moving from one apartment to another. But he found comfort and hope in sports. In high school, Iverson was a dual-sport athlete, excelling in both basketball and football.

Iverson faced a significant hurdle when he was involved in a bowling alley incident in high school, which led to him being sentenced to five years in prison. Fortunately, he was granted clemency after four months, but his dream of playing college basketball seemed over when top schools stopped recruiting him. However, Georgetown University gave him a chance, and Iverson took full advantage of it, standing out on the court and proving his worth.

When Iverson joined the NBA, being the first overall pick by the Philadelphia 76ers in the 1996 draft, he quickly made a name for himself. Standing at just six feet tall, he was often smaller than his opponents, but his heart was larger than most. Iverson was known for his speed, agility, and scoring ability, especially his iconic "crossover" dribble.

Despite his small stature, Iverson led the NBA in scoring four times and was an 11-time NBA All-Star. In 2001, he was named the league's Most Valuable Player (MVP) and carried the 76ers to the NBA Finals.

Off the court, Iverson was known for his unique style and individualism. He was one of the players responsible for popularizing tattoos and braids in the NBA. Despite controversies, he always stayed true to himself and was open about his struggles.

Iverson's journey to the top of the NBA is a story of overcoming adversity, staying true to oneself, and never giving up, no matter how big the challenge may seem. His story teaches kids that it's not about how many times you fall, but how many times you get back up.

Fun Facts:

Multi-Sport Athlete: In high school, Iverson was not only a basketball star but also the quarterback for the football team. He led both teams to Virginia state championships in his junior year.

"The Answer": Iverson's nickname is "The Answer." The moniker represents the idea that Iverson was the answer to the Philadelphia 76ers' struggles when he joined the team.

Iconic Crossover: One of Iverson's most iconic moments was his crossover dribble on Michael Jordan during his rookie year. This moment is a testament to Iverson's skill and fearlessness.

Scoring Machine: Iverson was known for his scoring ability. He led the NBA in scoring average four times during his career.

MVP Award: Despite being one of the shortest players in the league, Iverson proved that height doesn't determine success. He won the league MVP award in 2001, standing at just six feet tall.

Cultural Impact: Iverson had a significant impact on the culture of the NBA, popularizing trends like tattoos and cornrows, and influencing the league's dress code.

Number Retirement: The Philadelphia 76ers retired Iverson's number 3 jersey in a ceremony in 2014 to honor his contributions to the team.

Hall of Famer: Iverson was inducted into the Naismith Memorial Basketball Hall of Fame in 2016, cementing his legacy in the sport.

Allen Iverson's story teaches kids about resilience, individuality, and the belief in oneself. His story shows that no matter your background or size, with skill, determination, and hard work, you can reach great heights.

DIRK NOWITZKI

Born in Würzburg, Germany, Dirk initially pursued handball and tennis, even becoming a top-ranked junior tennis player in his region. However, he eventually fell in love with basketball, inspired by the success of German player Detlef Schrempf in the NBA.

Dirk wasn't immediately a star in the making. He was often overlooked because basketball wasn't as popular in Germany as other sports. However, his dedication to improvement was undeterred. His former coach, Holger Geschwindner, noticed Dirk's potential and rigorously trained him. He taught Dirk not only basketball skills but also about arts, sciences, and other wider world aspects, shaping Dirk as a well-rounded individual.

Dirk's hard work paid off when he was selected as the 9th overall pick in the 1998 NBA Draft by the Milwaukee Bucks and then immediately traded to the Dallas Mavericks. The transition to the NBA wasn't easy; Dirk struggled in his rookie season. Critics doubted whether he could compete at the NBA level, but he didn't let this deter him. Instead, he worked even harder to adapt his game to the intense competition.

Throughout his career, Dirk was known for his exceptional shooting ability, especially for a player of his height (7 ft 0 in). He revolutionized the power forward position with his unique shooting style, most notably his one-legged fadeaway jump shot, which became his trademark move and has since been adopted by many players.

With the Mavericks, Dirk led the team to 15 NBA Playoffs, including the franchise's first and only NBA Championship in 2011, where he also earned the Finals MVP award.

Known for his loyalty, Dirk spent his entire 21-season NBA career with the Mavericks, setting an NBA record for the most seasons with a single franchise.

Off the court, Dirk is known for his philanthropy, including the Dirk Nowitzki Foundation, which aims to help provide education, health, and well-being for children around the world.

Dirk Nowitzki's story is a perfect example of perseverance, dedication, loyalty, and the power of hard work. It shows that no matter where you come from or what obstacles you face, with the right mindset and dedication, you can achieve greatness.

Fun Facts:

German Roots: Dirk is one of the most successful international players in NBA history. He was born and raised in Würzburg, Germany, and is proud of his German heritage.

Tennis Player: Before focusing on basketball, Dirk was a talented tennis player in his youth, ranking at the top of his age group in Germany.

Unique Training: Dirk's longtime coach, Holger Geschwindner, emphasized a holistic approach to training. In addition to basketball, their sessions often included elements of art, science, and music.

One Club Man: Dirk spent his entire 21-year NBA career with the Dallas Mavericks, an example of his loyalty and dedication.

Revolutionary Style: Dirk revolutionized the power forward position with his shooting ability. His one-legged fadeaway jump shot has become iconic in the basketball world.

NBA Champion: In 2011, Dirk led the Mavericks to their first and only NBA Championship, earning the Finals MVP award for his outstanding performance.

30K Club: Dirk is one of only seven players in NBA history to score more than 30,000 points in their career.

NBA MVP: He was named the NBA's Most Valuable Player (MVP) in 2007, becoming the first European player to win the prestigious award.

Philanthropy: Dirk established the Dirk Nowitzki Foundation, which focuses on children's well-being, health, and education.

Hall of Famer: After his retirement, Dirk was inducted into the Naismith Memorial Basketball Hall of Fame, a testament to his influence on the sport.

Dirk Nowitzki's story is inspiring for kids, demonstrating that dedication, perseverance, and embracing one's unique abilities can lead to great success, regardless of where you come from.

James Naismith

Born in 1861 in Ontario, Canada, Naismith was not particularly outstanding in his early years. After losing both parents to typhoid fever at a young age, he was raised by his strict, religious aunt and uncle. As a young boy, he enjoyed playing a game called "Duck on a Rock," which would later influence the creation of basketball.

Naismith struggled academically in high school and took extra years to complete his coursework. He worked as a lumberjack for a while before deciding to focus on his physical education studies. Naismith earned a degree in physical education from McGill University in Montreal, where he excelled in sports.

In 1891, Naismith was studying to become a minister and working as an instructor at the International YMCA Training School in Springfield, Massachusetts. His supervisor, Dr. Luther Gulick, gave him a challenging task: invent a new game to occupy a "class of incorrigibles" — students who were bored with their regular physical education activities and too disruptive to be contained indoors during the harsh New England winter.

Naismith was given two weeks to come up with this new game. Drawing from his childhood game of "Duck on a Rock," he devised a game that involved throwing a ball into a basket, reducing the physical contact that occurred in games like football and rugby. He wrote down 13 basic rules, hung a peach basket onto the elevated track, and basketball was born.

The game was an instant success, and it quickly spread across the country and eventually the world. Naismith never sought profit or fame from his invention. He was more focused on his career in physical education and later, as the chaplain in the First Kansas Infantry during World War I.

Despite all the changes and adaptations over the years, the essence of Naismith's game has remained the same. His invention has inspired millions, creating a global platform that showcases athleticism, teamwork, and the spirit of fair competition. His story is a testament to the power of creativity, innovation, and persistence.

Fun Facts:

The Invention of Basketball: Naismith invented the game of basketball in 1891 while trying to create a new game to keep his gym class active on a rainy day. The first game was played with a soccer ball and two peach baskets.

The Original 13 Rules: The original rules of basketball, written by Naismith, did not include any guidelines about dribbling or the number of players on each team. The rules have evolved greatly since then.

Basketball's Spread: Naismith didn't patent basketball, nor did he profit from the game. He was more interested in physical education and saw the game as a way to help individuals develop physical and mental skills. He must have been proud to see the game spread rapidly and become a staple in YMCAs and schools within years of its creation.

First Basketball Coach: Naismith became the University of Kansas' first basketball coach in 1898, but his teams ironically ended up losing records. Despite this, he never lost his love for the game.

YMCA's Influence: As a physical education teacher at the YMCA International Training School in Massachusetts, Naismith had a significant impact on the spread of basketball through the YMCA channels, both nationally and internationally.

Lifetime Career: Besides inventing basketball, Naismith was a medical doctor and a minister, spending much of his career serving others in physical and spiritual health.

Basketball and Olympics: Naismith was able to see basketball adopted as an official event in the Summer Olympics in 1936 in Berlin, and he presented the medals to the winning teams.

Honoring Naismith: The Naismith Memorial Basketball Hall of Fame in Springfield, Massachusetts, is named in his honor, recognizing and honoring players, coaches, referees, and others who have made significant contributions to the game of basketball.

James Naismith's life and the invention of basketball demonstrate creativity, persistence, and dedication to physical education and fair play, providing a wonderful source of inspiration for kids.

MVP TROPHY

The NBA's Most Valuable Player (MVP) award is an inspiring symbol of hard work, dedication, and skill. This prestigious award is given annually to the player who contributes the most to their team's success during the regular season.

The MVP award was first given out for the 1955-56 season. Its first recipient was Bob Pettit of the St. Louis Hawks, who set an early standard for the qualities that make an MVP: leadership, a tireless work ethic, and the ability to elevate the performance of their team.

An inspiring story related to the MVP award is that of Steve Nash. Born in South Africa and raised in Canada, Nash wasn't initially considered an NBA prospect. Despite his talent, many scouts overlooked him due to his relative lack of height and athleticism compared to other players. Nash was eventually selected as the 15th pick in the 1996 NBA Draft by the Phoenix Suns, a selection that was booed by fans.

Despite the skepticism, Nash worked tirelessly to improve his skills. After two seasons with the Suns and six with the Dallas Mavericks, Nash returned to Phoenix and led the Suns to the best record in the NBA in the 2004-05 season. He won the MVP award that year and again in 2006, becoming just the ninth player in NBA history to win the award in back-to-back years.

Nash's story is a reminder that success doesn't always come immediately. Sometimes, it's about continually working hard, improving a little bit each day, and not getting discouraged when others doubt your abilities. His perseverance and dedication to his craft led him to become one of the most celebrated players in NBA history, proving that with hard work and determination, anyone can overcome the odds.

The MVP trophy isn't just about being the best player; it's about being the best teammate, leading by example, and making everyone around you better. It's a symbol of dedication, teamwork, and the relentless pursuit of excellence - values that can inspire kids in their endeavors, whether on the basketball court or in life.

Slam Dunks

The slam dunk is one of the most exciting and celebrated moves in basketball, known for its high energy and crowd-rousing nature. However, the story of how it came to be can serve as a source of inspiration for kids, showcasing the importance of creativity, innovation, and challenging the status quo.

Slam dunks weren't always a part of basketball. In fact, in the early days of the game, they were almost nonexistent. The game was more grounded, focused on passing and shooting with both feet planted on the floor.

Enter Darryl Dawkins, a young, energetic player with the Philadelphia 76ers in the 1970s. Standing at 6-foot-11, Dawkins had the height, but more importantly, he had the imagination. He became known for his powerful and flamboyant slam dunks, which he even started to name. There was the "Yo-Mama," the "Rim Wrecker," the "Look Out Below," and most famously, the "Chocolate-Thunder-Flying, Robinzine-Crying, Teeth-Shaking, Glass-Breaking, Rump-Roasting, Bun-Toasting, Wham-Bam, Glass-Breaker-I-Am-Jam." In fact, his dunks were so powerful that he shattered two backboards in the 1979 season, leading to changes in the way basketball rims were manufactured.

But it was not only the power of his dunks that was inspiring. Dawkins showed kids that basketball could be more than just a game of shooting and passing – it could be a spectacle, a show. He demonstrated the importance of flair, creativity, and putting your unique stamp on what you do.

Later players like Michael Jordan, Dominique Wilkins, and Vince Carter would further revolutionize the dunk, adding their unique twists, turns, and leaps. Today, the slam dunk is not just a move in basketball; it's a statement, an exclamation point on a play. It's a way for players to express their creativity, athleticism, and personality on the court.

The story of the slam dunk teaches kids to think outside the box, not be afraid to add their personal flair to the things they do, and continually push boundaries to innovate and excel. Just as Darryl Dawkins and those who came after him changed the game of basketball, kids can make a significant impact in their own fields when they apply creativity, passion, and the courage to do things their own way.

REVIEW

Hello, extraordinary reader,

As you close this book and reflect on the stories of resilience, determination, and triumph that unfolded on the basketball court, we hope you're feeling inspired. Perhaps you're even lacing up your sneakers and practicing your layups, or sharing these tales of courage and tenacity with friends and family.

We believe that these stories, just like the best passes in a thrilling basketball game, are meant to be shared. That's why we're reaching out to ask you a small favor. If you've enjoyed "Dribble, Shoot, Grow" would you consider leaving a review?

Your thoughts and reflections matter immensely. By sharing your review, you're not just giving us feedback, but you're also helping these stories reach more readers—more budding basketball stars, more dreamers, and more champions in the making. Your words could encourage a child to pick up this book, and in doing so, inspire them to believe in their potential, chase their dreams, and play their own game of life with determination and joy.

Your reviews will be our assist, helping us score a three-pointer in the game of inspiring more kids. Just as the best basketball players elevate their teams, your insights can lift up and inspire a whole new generation of readers.

If you could take a few minutes to leave a review, we'd be deeply grateful. Whether it's a few sentences or a detailed breakdown, every word counts. Share what you loved, what inspired you, and perhaps even how these stories might have sparked a change in your own game.

Thank you for joining us on this journey through "Dribble, Shoot, Grow" We can't wait to read your thoughts, and more importantly, we can't wait for others to be encouraged by the enthusiasm and inspiration you pass along.

Keep reaching for the stars, keep playing the game with all your heart, and remember—you're a part of this amazing team, too!

With gratitude and a high-five,

Inspiring Winning Stories